MICK MANNING and BRITA GRANSTRÖM have won many awards for their picture information books, including the Smarties Silver Award and the English Association Award. In 2013, their huge contribution to children's literature was recognised with a nomination for the prestigious Astrid Lindgren Memorial Award, the largest international children's and young adult literature award in the world. Their books for Frances Lincoln include *The Beatles, Charles Dickens: Scenes from an Extraordinary Life, What Mr Darwin Saw, Tail-End Charlie, Taff in the WAAF, The Secrets of Stonehenge, Dino-Dinners, Woolly Mammoth*, the Fly on the Wall series: *Roman Fort, Viking Longship, Pharaoh's Egypt* and *Greek Hero, Nature Adventures* and *Wild Adventures*. They have four sons, and divide their time between the North of England and Brita's homeland of Sweden. Find out more about their books at www.mickandbrita.com.

For Janetta and Jude

Front endpaper
In 851 AD two young friends, Grim and Ylva, visit a Viking
rune stone on the island of Gotland.

Back endpaper
In 882 AD, Thora and Thorkel play hide-and-seek around Uggla's
memorial stone in Yorkshire.

Title page (background) and back cover
An image from a rune stone showing the Viking hero Sigurd killing
the dragon, Fafnir.

Researched on location in Jorvik, Dublin, Northumberland
and Scandinavia.

Archaeological consultant: Dr Richard Hall. Dr Hall directed
the Viking dig in York and helped create the Jorvik Centre.
He is Director of Archaeology at York Archaeological Trust.

Find out more about this book at www.mickandbrita.com

No living creatures were harmed during the making of this book.

Fly On The Wall: Viking Longship copyright © Frances Lincoln Limited 2006
Text and illustrations copyright © Mick Manning and Brita Granström 2006

First published in Great Britain in 2006 and in the USA in 2007
by Frances Lincoln Children's Books, 74-77 White Lion Street
London N1 9PF

www.franceslincoln.com

Distributed in the USA by Publishers Group West

This edition first published in Great Britain in 2015

British Library Cataloguing in Publication Data
available on request

ISBN 13: 978-1-84780-624-6

Printed in China

9 8 7 6 5 4 3 2 1

F

FRANCES LINCOLN
CHILDREN'S BOOKS

VIKING LONGSHIP

MICK MANNING
BRITA GRANSTRÖM

Consultant: Dr Richard Hall,
York Archaeological Trust

CONTENTS

Who were the Vikings? 6

Meet the Vikings 7

Dragging a Dragon 8

Smash and Grab 10

Storm at Sea 12

Shipyard 14

Warrior Training 16

Sacrifice 18

Invasion 20

Battlefield 22

Viking Farm 24

Viking Women 26

Jorvik 28

Yule Feast 30

Raiders 32

Viking Funeral 34

End of the Vikings 36

What the Vikings left behind 36

Glossary and Index 36

Who were the Vikings?

'Viking' was originally a name given to the sea-pirates from the Scandinavian countries of Denmark, Sweden and Norway. In 793 AD, Viking pirates raided the monastery at Lindisfarne. The Christian monks were the only people writing books in those days, and they were horrified. They described all Vikings as bloodthirsty barbarians, although Vikings were probably no more violent than the Saxons and other peoples of the age. At this time England was divided into many small kingdoms and their Anglo-Saxon kings fought one another for power. England was a Christian country, but the Saxons had once worshipped the same pagan gods as the Vikings.

As they became more organised Vikings grouped together, sailing and exploring further. Waves of Vikings colonised parts of England, Scotland, Ireland and Europe in the 9th, 10th and 11th centuries. Their major settlement in England was the town of Jorvik (York).

Other Vikings sailed east, settling in parts of Russia. They traded and raided as far south as the Byzantine Empire. Others migrated north, colonising Iceland and Greenland – some Vikings even went on to discover North America. So Vikings were much more than pirates – they were skilful boat-builders, sailors, explorers, traders, craftsmen, clever farmers and poets.

ICELAND

NORWAY

Gokstad

SWEDEN

Uppsala

Birka

SCOTLAND

Lindisfarne

Northumbria

Jorvik

IRELAND

Dublin

Wales

Dane

Mercia

law

East Anglia

border

Wessex

London

DENMARK

Hedeby

FRANCE

Paris

Meet the Vikings

Our story begins in 864, and follows the life of a beautiful 9th century Viking Longship and the Vikings who sailed in her. Let's look in on some of them and see how they lived their lives in those dangerous times...

YLVA
Grim's wife

GRIM
a Viking warrior

THORA and THORKEL
Grim's children

UGGLA
Grim's best friend

RAGNAR
a Viking rover

ESKIL
a Saxon priest

HILDA
a priestess

INGEBORG
Ragnar's widow

EARL HALFDAN
a leader of the Great Army

Dragging a Dragon

Here comes a longship! Dragged overland between river and sea, this dragon belongs to a pirate – a Viking called Ragnar.

Look!

The thunder god is throwing his magic hammer!

Ragnar has named his ship *The Sea Dragon*.

A small Viking longship is light enough to drag overland. This sort of shortcut is called 'portage'.

The word 'Viking' probably comes from the word 'Vik' meaning inlet. It could be that they sailed from

Portage meant that Vikings could carry their boat between seas and rivers for short distances.

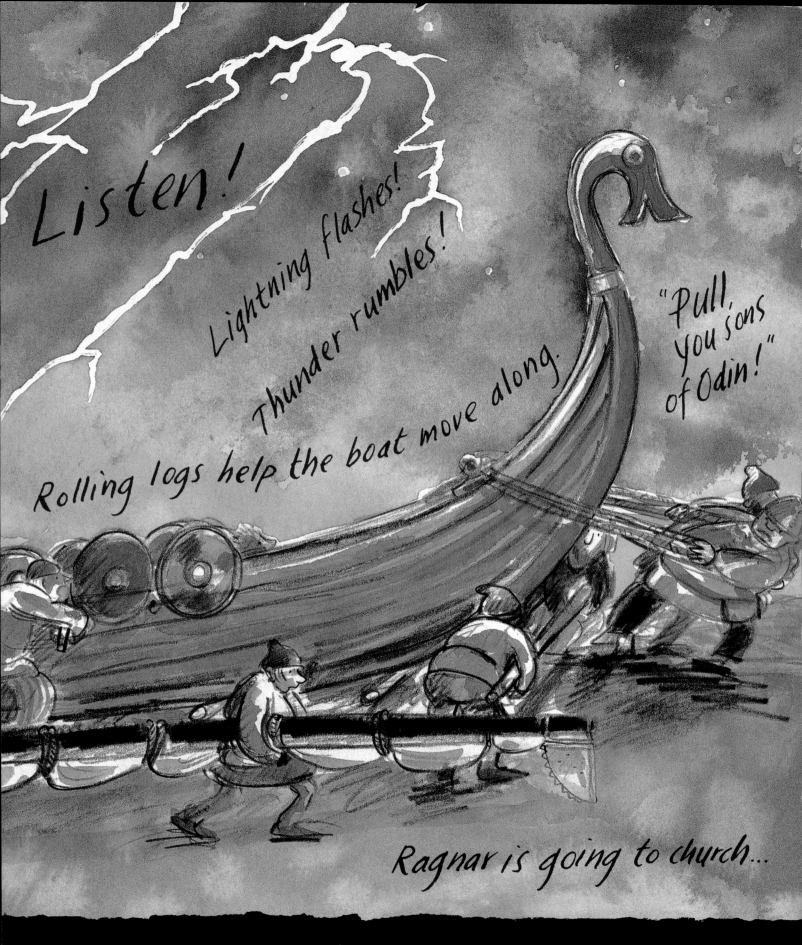

Viking ships were shallow enough to sail up a river but strong enough to cross an ocean.

We know about Viking ships from carved picture stones and the remains of beautiful longships discovered in Scandinavia.

...This Irish church burns quickly.

Fancy clasps, hinges and pages are torn from the monks' handmade books.

pages blowing in the wind

'OX' can carry a monk under his arm.!

chests

silver cups and plates

water barrel

cloth

In 793, the English monastery of Lindisfarne was burned and all the valuables stolen. It was the first of many attacks across Britain, Ireland and Europe.

Silver and gold was usually hacked into chunks to share out among the crew. It was called 'hack silver'.

Smash and Grab

Ragnar's no Christian – but he likes to go to church!
Surprise! Surprise! Crash and burn! Smash and grab!
Stealing silver is this sea-wolf's work!

"Take everything valuable. Burn the rest!"

The monks are too shocked to struggle. They will be sold as slaves.

Slaves were the bottom level of society, bought and sold like animals. They could even be killed or sacrificed by their masters.

Silver decorations from the covers of church books have been found in Viking settlements. They had been made into jewellery!

Storm at Sea

On the way home a storm lashes down. Waves swamp the decks. Ragnar is washed overboard into Ran's net. He's been drowned by the gods! After a week lost at sea, the longship drifts into harbour – wrecked!

This sail is made of wool.

shields

The 'steering board' steers the ship.

Each member of the crew sits on his sea-chest.

Niord, the god of the sea, could give a safe voyage or a bad one! Vikings believed in a family of gods ruled by Odin, the 'All Father'.

An eagle-giant called Corpse Swallower was thought to live at the edge of the world. It was believed that storm winds were made by his wing beats!

Even Viking ships can't cope with waves like these!

The sail is in tatters!

The treasure goes overboard with Ragnar.

captured monks

Hold on tight or you'll never see land again!

A Viking harbour in Denmark.

jetty

Vikings believe in Ran – a sea-demon who drowns sailors in a fishing net.

Shipyard

Two young Vikings, Grim and Uggla, buy the broken longship from Ragnar's widow. Keen for adventure, they repair the damage, carefully healing *The Sea Dragon*'s wounds with a ship builder's skill.

A new ship is being built here.

scraping wood

Waterproofing: filling the gaps with wool and tar – it smells of kippers!

Wooden clamp holds wood in position.

Grim hammers in ship rivets.

Uggla is a nickname. It means 'Owl'. His real name is Uggleberd.

Fresh 'green' timber was best for boat-building as it was soft to cut and didn't split like dry, seasoned timber.

Oak, or sometimes pine, was used for the keel and planking. It took about 12 big trees to make one longship.

Grim haggles with Ragnar's widow, Ingeborg.
"It's worth much.!"

"It's worth nowt.!"

The boat must be ready SOON — Earl Halfdan has promised the Vikings a great adventure!

Tor is trimming new planks.

Toke is drilling holes in the planks.

Vikings are skilled ship builders.

Wood shavings get everywhere!

Tests on the timbers of one Danish longship show that it was built in Ireland.

Sails were made of wool, and ropes were made of hemp, walrus or seal hide. Glue was made from pine resin and fat.

Warrior Training

Working for Earl Halfdan is well paid! But swordsmanship and battle skills can't be taught overnight. Yet they must learn fast. The invasion of England is about to begin!

sword

Aaaah!

spear

colourful shields to show in battle.

Uggla is a fierce warrior. He is teaching the new recruits how to make a shield wall...

The 3-point plan on joining the Great Army was:

Many recruits were farmers, craftsmen and merchants

The young twins Freaki and Geri, are quick to learn.

Big Orm is a slow learner - but he tries hard!

Grim has spent all his savings on war gear.

Grim and Uggla know how to fight. Grim is to be one of Halfdan's captains.

helmet

silver brooch

cloak

sword

knife

belt

chain mail

scabbard

wool trousers

leather boots

A Viking's weapons included the battle-axe, sword, shield and spear.

A new sword was very expensive so many warriors made do with second-hand swords, traded or claimed after battle.

"Odin... Odin... Odin...
Odin... Odin... Odin..."

Grim and Uggla sacrifice a chicken.

Vikings worship outside.

Vikings believed the gods would help them if they were offered gifts as sacrifices.

Thor fought evil giants with his magic hammer. Vikings wore pendants shaped like hammers for good luck.

Sacrifice

By the old oak, where the gods look down, Grim and Uggla make a sacrifice. In this wild place, open to the sky, they ask for Thor's strength, Odin's cunning and Frey's blessing.

The skins of sacrificed animals hang from the branches.

Odin's ravens, Hugin and Munin, tell him what goes on in the world.

Hilda splashes blood on the statues!

Thor has a magic hammer called Mjollnir.

The Viking gods live in a place called Asgard.

Frey
Lord of growing things, harvest and peace.

Odin
Father of the gods. Creator of the world!

Thor
Mighty son of Odin! The people's friend.

To country folk, Frey was the most important god. His sister, Freya, rode a chariot pulled by cats. Her followers used magic called *seid*.

Frigg, the wife of Odin, was the goddess of home and motherhood. She spun the clouds on her magic loom!

Vikings unload the supplies from a knarr.

The horses look pleased to see dry land!

A knarr is a sturdy cargo ship.

uggla

Longships can be dragged up on to beaches and sail up rivers too.

Different peoples lived in Britain at this time. They included Saxons, Angles, Britons, Picts and Scots.

King Edmund of East Anglia did a deal with the Vikings and gave them supplies and extra horses. But they still killed him a few years later!

Invasion

The Sea Dragon is one of many longships dragged up on the sandy shore, spilling out men, supplies, weapons and horses. Earl Halfdan climbs the wind-blown sand dunes, shouting a battle cry to his men.

"The Vikings are here!"

Grim

Odin's ravens

Halfdan is a wealthy earl. He wears rich clothes, jewellery and furs.

England was divided into small squabbling kingdoms. They were no match for the Viking Great Army when it invaded in 865.

Earl Halfdan was one of many leaders of the Great Army. Others included Guthrum, Anund, Oscytel and Ivar 'the boneless'!

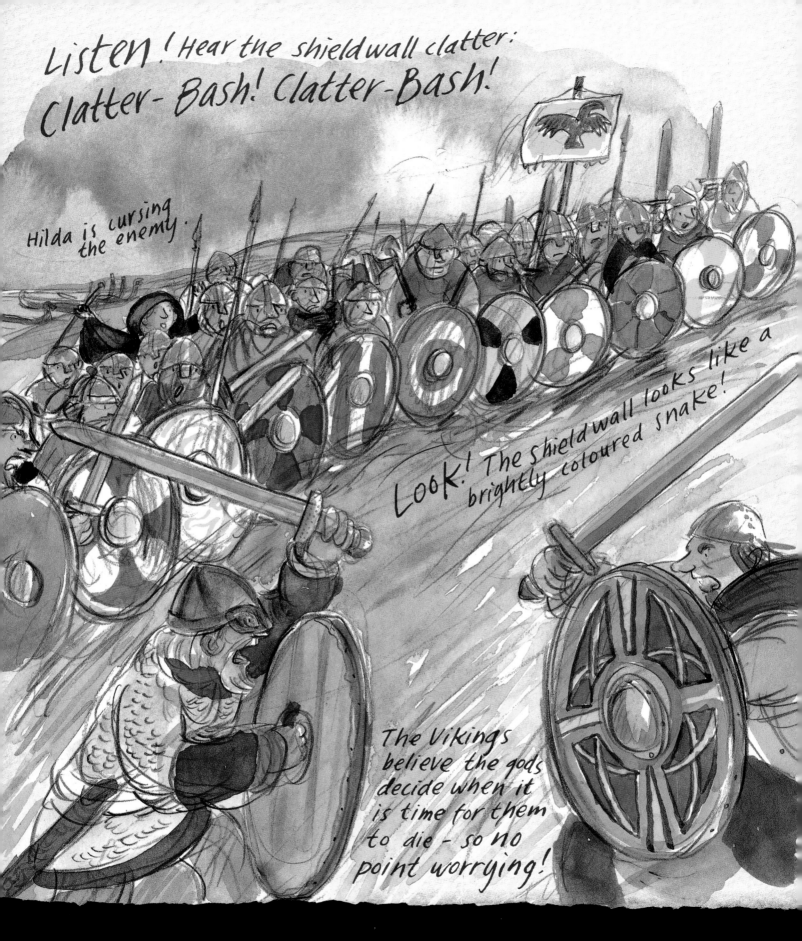

Listen! Hear the shieldwall clatter:
Clatter-Bash! Clatter-Bash!

Hilda is cursing the enemy.

Look! The shieldwall looks like a brightly coloured snake!

The Vikings believe the gods decide when it is time for them to die - so no point worrying!

Vikings believed Odin's warrior-maidens called Valkyries carried dead warriors to Valhall which means 'hall of the slain'.

Vikings believed they died because Odin needed them to fight at the battle of Ragnarok against giants and monsters.

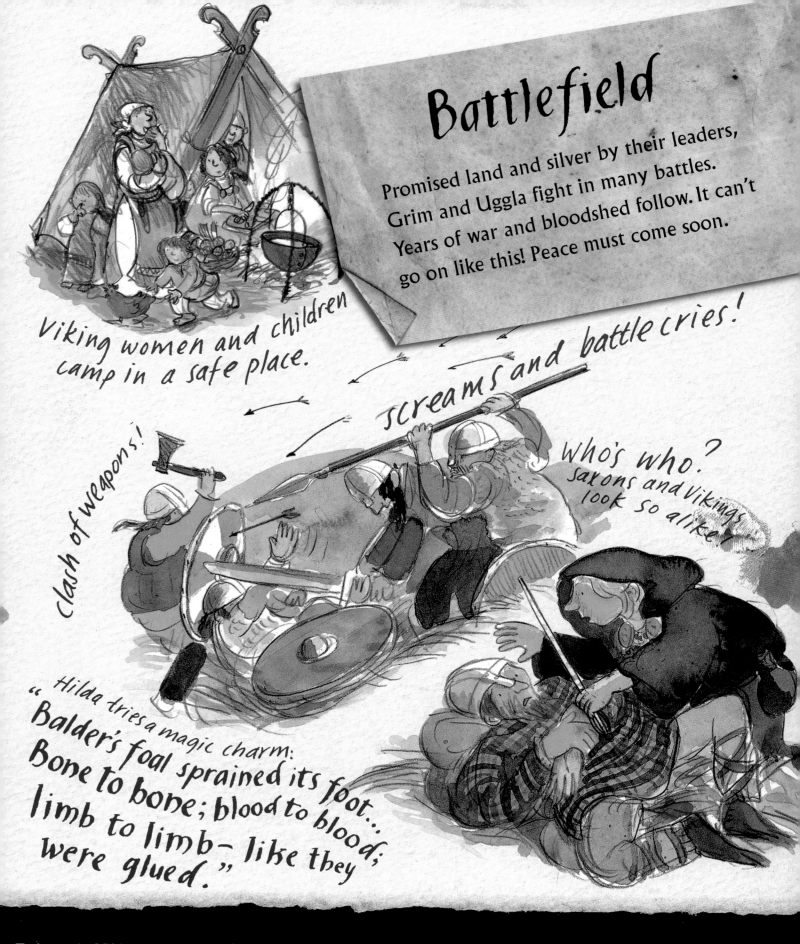

Battlefield

Promised land and silver by their leaders,
Grim and Uggla fight in many battles.
Years of war and bloodshed follow. It can't
go on like this! Peace must come soon.

Viking women and children camp in a safe place.

screams and battle cries!

clash of weapons!

who's who?
Saxons and Vikings
look so alike!

Hilda tries a magic charm:
"Balder's foal sprained its foot... Bone to bone; blood to blood; limb to limb – like they were glued."

To keep the Vikings away, many Saxon kingdoms paid them large amounts of silver.

King Alfred's West Saxons fought back. Their victory in 878 made the Vikings agree to a treaty sharing England between them.

With Vikings now ruling Jorvik, many have settled down in the north and east of England.

Ylva and Grim can see the whole of their land from the roof. The farm is near the river. They can sail to Jorvik from here.

Jorvik (York) was the cosmopolitan capital of Viking England. People came from far and wide to trade.

Many Viking place names such as *thwaite* (clearing), *toft* (farm), *carr* (marsh), *gate* (road) and *by* (farm)

Grim is fixing the roof.

People live in this end.

Animals live in this end.

Farmyard smells – pig manure, goats, woodsmoke!

Thorkel and Thora often play with Saxon children.

"Leyk" means play.
"Hi" means hello.

POO! The toilet is just a hole in the ground.

Viking Farm

Grim has put away his sword and shield. Spade and plough are his weapons of war. He fights with weeds! Battles against rocks! Nowadays *The Sea Dragon* carries horn-headed warriors. Uggla's loading an army of goats!

Because these place names occur alongside Saxon ones, it shows that Vikings lived peacefully with the locals.

Viking children didn't go to school. They learned skills from their family and friends.

Vikings consider men and women as equal.

smoky!

The only 'window' is the hole in the roof. The Vikings call it 'vindeye'.

A slave boy brings wood.

Ylva weaves cloth on the loom.

Thora learns how to spin wool with her granny.

Viking women had more rights than women in many other countries. They could own land, divorce and inherit property.

An Irish Viking woman called Aud migrated with her family to Iceland. She was one of Iceland's most important settlers.

Viking Women

Ylva Ormsdottir is a clever woman. She runs the farm, decides what's to be done in the longhouse, barn, storeroom and henhouse – Ylva rules the roost!

people sleep on benches along the walls.

Ylva sings while she is baking.

Birka Bread:

200g (1¾cups) flour. 100g (1cup) oats. ½ tsp salt ½ tsp cumin. 50g (½cup) butter. 50g (½cup) honey 200 ml (¾ cup) water.

① Mix the dry ingredients together.
② Rub in the soft butter until the mixture is crumbly.
③ Add honey and water ④ Mix to a dough.
⑤ Roll into a fat sausage. ⑥ Chill for 1 hour.
⑦ Slice into ½ cm (¼ in) slices.
⑧ Cook in a dry frying pan until golden.

The hens wander indoors too!

Granny is ironing with a glass smoother on a whale bone 'ironing' board.

Women could be market traders, priestesses and farmers. One woman was a rune carver and Irish tales even tell of wild warrior women.

When the men were away raiding or trading, the women took charge of the farm and workers.

Jorvik

All along the smelly quayside, different ships bob at anchor. Grim takes a walk down Koppa Gata and buys a comb there for his nits! Ylva's bought a string of beads and some wooden toys.

Jorvik is a noisy, smoky place.

cupmaker

noble man

weighing scales

woodencups

baskets

antler and bone

Thorfast is a comb maker. He scratches runes on his combs: "Thorfast makes a good comb!"

Viking buildings were usually made of wood, wattle and daub. They were roofed with straw, reeds or sometimes wooden tiles.

Leather shoes, cups, bowls, jewellery and combs were made and traded by the craftspeople in towns like York, Dublin in Ireland, and Birka in Sweden.

Vikings have their own coins minted.

wolf hair

It's a place to exchange gossip...

... or fall in love!

People from faraway places are here to buy and sell.

Vikings write with runes. This is the runic alphabet called Futhark.

f u th a r k : h n i a s : t b m l R

Runes can be scratched or carved on skin, bone, wood or stone — the Vikings don't use paper.

Moneyers made coins by hammering a blank metal disc on to a metal 'die' that pressed a special design into it.

Everyone had nits (headlice) and fleas, and finds of Jorvik poo prove they were infested with tapeworms too. The drinking wells were too close to the toilets!

In one story, Frey is given a magic ship. In another, Odin murders a giant and then creates the world from its body parts!

Yule was a midwinter feast. There were 12 days of eating, drinking and worshipping. Today, it is still celebrated – but we call it Christmas!

Yule Feast

Grim hosts a Yule feast for friends and neighbours. His stories of Thor make the priest laugh out loud. Tales about Odin make everyone nervous – people glance over their shoulder when they hear about him.

Grim tells a story about the gods:

"I've stolen Thor's hammer" yells the giant Thrym. "If you want it back, let me marry goddess Freya!" Thor puts on Freya's dress, covers his beard with a veil and goes to the wedding. Thrym, thinking he's married Freya, wants a kiss. Thor snatches back his mighty hammer – "KISS THIS!" he shouts!

Every night the gods feasted on *Sahrimner*, a magic pig that came back to life each day.

Vikings used skis and bone-skates to hunt and play in wintertime. Feasts and festivals cheered up the

West Saxons torch the roof... then wait outside, weapons ready.

The Vikings sneak out the back.

The thatch is alight!

"Fight me!"

Brave Uqqla gives his friends valuable time to escape.

As years passed the Great Army split up. Some settled down in the north. Other groups fought on in the south or went raiding to Ireland and France.

By 917, the West Saxons once again ruled East Anglia and the Midlands but hadn't conquered Northumbria and its major settlement, Jorvik.

Raiders

Saxon raiders attack in the darkness. Smoking out Viking settlers like rats from a haystack. Grim and his followers grab rusty weapons. They break down the wall, escape in the smoke. Run to the river, down to their longship. Row for their lives while arrows rain down!

smoke in everyone's eyes   goats bleat   children cry

chickens cluck   dogs bark

They'll be back after the raiders have gone.

Luckily it's hard to aim arrows by moonlight.

They escape up the river where they have friends—
but someone is missing.

The Anglo-Saxon Chronicle, a history book written at the time, records many big battles and small raids: Saxons v Danes, Danes v Norse-Irish and so on.

One page reads: "West Saxons went forth on the enemy's tracks, hewing them from behind with blades new sharpened."

Uggla is to be given a hero's send off.

Grim shouts a verse: "The shield of the house has sailed out in Death's darkness to a dearer place..."

Men and women are buried with the belongings they need in the next life: tools, dogs, weapons... sometimes even slaves!

Everyone believes Uggla will soon be feasting in Valhall.

Many Vikings hoped to go to Valhall, the hall of Odin. Others looked forward to Freya's hall, Sessrumnir, or Thrudheim, the hall of mighty Thor.

Legend tells that when killed by the trickery of Loki, Balder, darling of the gods, was pushed out to sea in a burning boat.

Viking Funeral

Uggla the owl, killed by an arrow, is placed in the earth surrounded by gifts. At the funeral feast, the longship is burned. But Grim doesn't believe death is the end! Above the crackling flames he roars a farewell to his old friend.

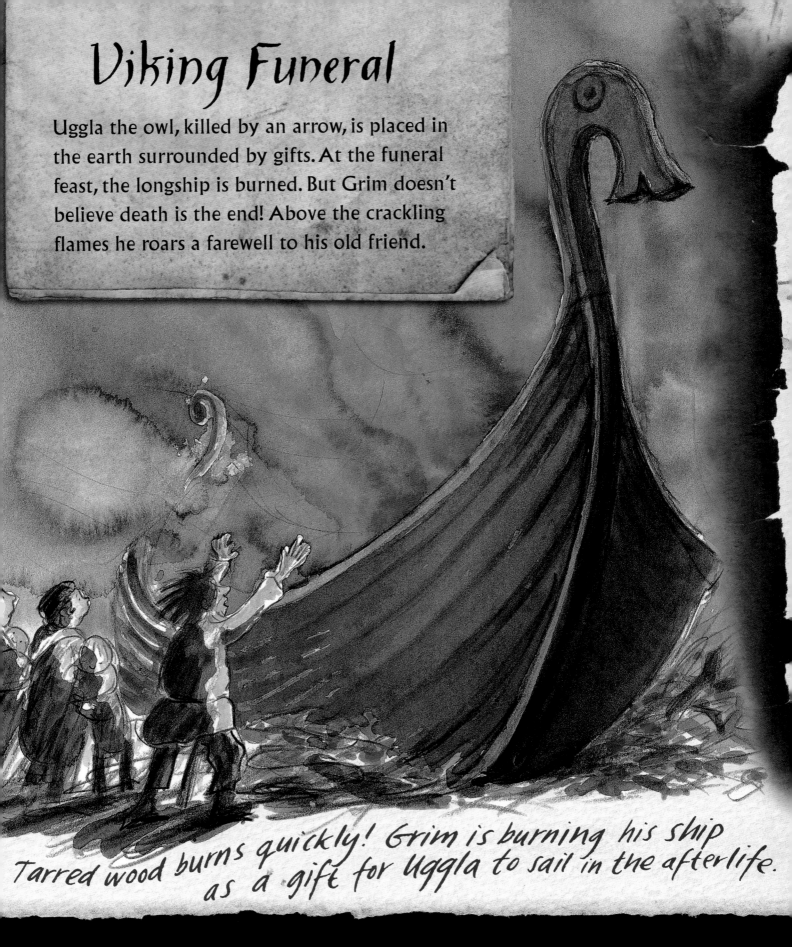

Tarred wood burns quickly! Grim is burning his ship as a gift for Uggla to sail in the afterlife.

Vikings could be buried with bits of boats, in boat-shaped graves or even cremated. Their possessions, buried with them, tell us a lot about their lives.

Despite all the bloodshed and wars life went on. Anglo-Scandinavian farmers had to rebuild and begin again.

End of the Vikings

The Vikings conquered much of England, and parts of Scotland, Ireland and Wales. They traded and raided from these new bases.

When the Viking's Great Army invaded England in 865 AD, only the West Saxons led by King Alfred were not beaten. After many battles, a treaty was signed with Alfred, which recognised the Vikings' rule over the north and east of England. This area became known as the Danelaw. Viking leaders handed out land to their followers and many Vikings settled and became farmers, marrying with the local Saxons and Angles. Today, historians call these people Anglo-Scandinavians.

But for almost 200 years there were power struggles between the Saxons, the Anglo-Scandinavians, the Scots and the Irish Viking colonies. In 1016, Cnut the Great, a Christian Viking, became one of England's most famous kings by uniting Scandinavia and England and ruling wisely for many years. But when he died, his empire fell apart and the West Saxons once again became England's rulers. In 1066, King Harold and his Anglo-Scandinavian army beat off a Norwegian invasion, only to be beaten themselves a few weeks later at Hastings by William the Conqueror and his Norman knights. The Normans were themselves descendants of Vikings who had settled in France 150 years earlier – but that's another story!

What the Vikings left behind

Thousands of English words like 'egg', 'window', 'knife' and 'law' come from Viking languages. So do many greetings like 'hi' and 'hey' and surnames ending in 'son'.

Some days of the week are named after the Viking's pagan gods: Tyr's day, Wodin's (Odin's) day, Thor's day and Frey day.

Many Europeans (including European settlers who went to Australia and America) have Viking blood in their veins.

Remains of Viking objects, ships and settlements can be found in museums and visitors centres like York, Dublin, Roskilde in Denmark, Oslo in Norway, Birka in Sweden and L'Anse aux Meadows in Newfoundland – so why not explore the lives of Vikings and their longships yourself?

Glossary & Index

Anglo–Saxons (pg 6 and 33)   The people living in England at the time of the Viking invasions included Saxons, Angles and Jutes. They were originally from Germany and Denmark and had themselves invaded England around 500 AD.

Anglo–Scandinavians (pg 35 and 36)   What historians call the mixed population of Vikings and Anglo-Saxons living in the north and east of England from the 10th century.

Asgard (pg 19)   Home of the Viking gods

Balder (pg 23 and 34)   Son of Odin. God of beauty and light.

Britons (pg 20)   Also known as Welsh and Celts. The people still living in Wales, and parts of southern Scotland at this time.

Byzantine Empire (pg 6)   A huge wealthy empire centred around Greece and the eastern mediterranean countries.

Danes   What the writers at the time called the Vikings of the Great Army who were mostly from Denmark. Some Viking settlers also came from Sweden and Norway, and fought in the wars.

Danelaw (pg 36)   What the area of England settled by the Viking invaders eventually came to be called.

East Anglia (pg 20 and 32)   A kingdom originally founded by the East Angles.

Frey (pg 19, 30 and 34)   The nature god who made the earth

Grim will never forget The Sea Dragon and Ylva is going to pay for a memorial stone for Uggla.

Freya (pg 19 and 31) Goddess of fertility and magic, and the sister of Frey.

Frigg (pg 19) Goddess of motherhood and wife of Odin.

Futhark (pg 29) The Viking alphabet of runes.

Great Army (pg 7, 16, 21, 32 and 36) The organised alliance of Viking leaders and their warriors who invaded England in 865 AD.

Hemp (pg 15) A plant with strong fibres that can be twisted for rope-making.

Jorvik (pg 24, 28, 29 and 32) The major settlement of Viking England, now called York. Amazing archaeological discoveries can be seen at Jorvik Viking Centre and online at www.jorvik-viking-centre.co.uk

Koppa Gata (pg 28) The street of cup-makers. The original name for Coppergate, still a street in York to this day.

Knarr (pg 20) Cargo ships that carried supplies and settlers to Britain, Iceland and Greenland – and probably to North America, which the Vikings discovered and named Vinland.

Longhouse (pg 27) A Viking farmhouse.

Loki (pg 34) A trickster god with winged shoes. He eventually betrayed the gods, joining the forces of evil in a ship made of old fingernails called Naglfar.

Niord (pg 12) Father of Frey and Freya and a nature god of the sea and weather.

Normans (pg 36) The Normans were descendants of Vikings who had settled in Normandy, France.

Nits and fleas (pg 28 and 29) Blood-sucking insects living on the human body.

Norse (pg 33) Vikings from Norway who settled mostly in Ireland and Scotland, Cumbria and Merseyside.

Odin (pg 12, 19, 22, 30 and 31) Also called 'All Father' by the Vikings, Odin was the creator of the world – god of war and death as well as poetry and wisdom. Odin's wife is Frigg.

Pagan (pg 30) A general name for people who were not Christians but worshipped nature and had more than one god.

Picts (pg 20) The people who lived in the north of Scotland at the time.

Portage (pg 8) Carrying a longship short distances overland.

Priestess (pg 7 and 27) Viking religion wasn't very organised but priestesses or 'Volva' used magic charms.

Ragnarok (pg 22) The final battle between the gods and the forces of evil led by Loki. Both sides and the entire world would be destroyed. But a new world would arise and Balder would return to rule it.

Seid (pg 19) Pronounced *say–the*, this is a sort of witchcraft practised by the priestesses who worshipped Freya.

Tapeworms (pg 29) These were very common in those days and were swallowed as eggs in dirty drinking water. They grow and live in the human body.

Thor (pg 19, 31 and 34) The most popular of the Viking gods. He fought evil with his magic hammer and righted wrongs. Many Vikings wore a hammer symbol round their neck for good luck.

Ugglebarnby (pg 24) A village in Yorkshire. It's named after a Viking called Uggleberd.

Valhall (pg 22 and 34) The hall of the dead where Viking warriors killed in battle went to party until it was time to fight at Ragnarok.

Valkyries (pg 22) Odin's warrior-maidens who carried slain warriors from the battlefield to Valhall. Thor's daughter, Thrud, was one of many Valkyrie.

Viking stories (pg 31) The Vikings told many exciting, scary, rude and funny stories about their gods. We know about many of them from a book called *The Edda*.

Wattle and daub (pg 28) Woven willow branches daubed with

FLY ON THE WALL · see history as it happened

Have you read the other Fly On The Wall books?

VIKING LONGSHIP
MICK MANNING & BRITA GRANSTRÖM

ROMAN FORT
MICK MANNING & BRITA GRANSTRÖM

PHARAOH'S EGYPT
MICK MANNING & BRITA GRANSTRÖM

GREEK HERO
MICK MANNING & BRITA GRANSTRÖM

See how the mummy-makers perform their grisly work and sail down the Nile in *Pharaoh's Egypt*. Patrol with a windswept centurion, eavesdrop in the smelly toilets and dine at a tasty banquet in *Roman Fort*. Watch skilful ship builders at work, visit a Viking farmstead and charge into battle in *Viking Longship*, and follow a Greek soldier to the Olympics in *Greek Hero*.

These books are packed with up-to-date information, detailed drawings and colourful characters, so you can be a fly on the wall and see history as it happened!

'The sketchbook format has an energy and warmth which really brings history to life.' – *Books for Keeps*

'This book and others in the series deserve to be placed with the best history books for young learners.' – *English Association Magazine* on *Greek Hero*

Contents

Anglo-Saxon Britain 4

Who was in charge? 6

Where would I live? 8

What would my childhood be like? 10

What clothes would I wear? 12

What would I eat and drink? 14

How would I have fun? 16

What would I believe? 18

What would I do when I grew up? 20

How could I become a warrior? 22

After the Anglo-Saxons 24

How do we know? 26

Map 28

Quiz 29

Glossary 30

Find out more 31

Index 32

Some words are shown in bold, **like this**. You can find out what they mean by looking in the glossary.

Anglo-Saxon Britain

From around AD 400, warriors from Europe began to invade Britain. They sailed across the North Sea, looking for new lands to settle in. They are now known as the Anglo-Saxons.

Before the Anglo-Saxons arrived, southern Britain was part of the Roman **Empire**. The Roman army left Britain in AD 410, leaving the way open for new settlers. The Anglo-Saxons were a mixture of people from lands that are now Germany, Denmark, and the Netherlands. Gradually, they took over most of England, dividing it into seven kingdoms. They pushed the **Celtic** Britons into Wales, Scotland, and Cornwall.

TIME OF INVASION

Around AD 400	Anglo-Saxons begin to settle in Britain
AD 597	St Augustine brings Christianity to Britain
Around AD 600	Seven Anglo-Saxon kingdoms created
AD 793	First recorded attack by Viking raiders
AD 886	Alfred the Great becomes King of Wessex
1042	Edward the Confessor becomes king of all England
1066	Battle of Hastings; Norman forces conquer England